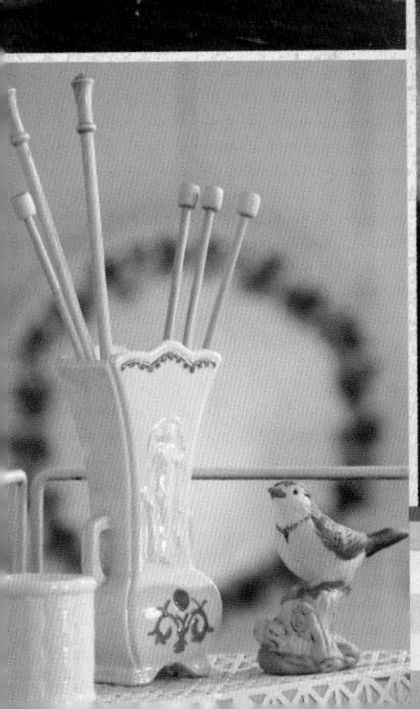

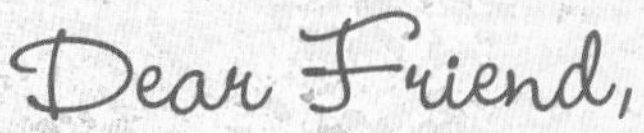

Knitting is such a wonderful pastime ... ce when your projects work up quickly and easily, like these twelve patterns. Just look at some of the special things you can create...a wrap blooming with flowering vines, an oh-so-sweet teddy bear, a warm sweater for your dog and a colorful felted purse. Make these designs for friends, family, or yourself. You'll be surprised how fast you finish each one.

Knit up some fun!

Vickie & Jo Ann

LEISURE ARTS, INC
Little Rock, AR

Felted Purse

Fun colors and a wonderful texture make this felted purse so nice to have. Because you hold two strands of yarn together while knitting, it works up quicker than you might think!

Instructions on page 12

Clutch

If you haven't tried felting yet, this pretty and practical clutch is a great place to start. At 5"x7", it's just the right size to hold small necessities. Use a big button from your grandmother's sewing basket, or find one at a flea market.

Instructions on page 14

Textured Purse

Just imagine this shoulder bag knitted in your favorite color of bulky weight yarn. The purse is lined with fabric, so it can hold everything from knitting needles to car keys.

Instructions on page 15

Textured Stripes Afghan

This restful afghan is knitted with two strands of yarn, so you get a beautiful blanket in a hurry!

Instructions on page 17

Dog Sweater

Spend just a little time knitting this sweater for your best pal, and he (or she) can wear it for many cool seasons to come.

Instructions on page 18

Flowered Stole

Oh-so-pretty flowers bloom on this stole all season long. The knitted blossoms and I-cord vines are fun to arrange and sew on as you wish.

Instructions on page 19

Hat

The flower is optional on this quick-to-knit hat.

Instructions on page 21

Mittens

Following our directions for children and adult sizes, you can knit these wonderful mittens for everyone you know!

Instructions on page 22

Toe Up Socks

Treat someone you love to a pair of soft, thick socks to wear around the house! The directions include three sizes for women.

Instructions on page 23

Blue Booties

A precious baby boy you know needs these little blue booties. Knit them up in just one or two evenings.

Pink Booties

Perfectly pink booties for her sweet, tiny feet. She can wear them now, and save them for her own daughter to wear one day.

Instructions for the Blue and Pink Booties begin on page 25

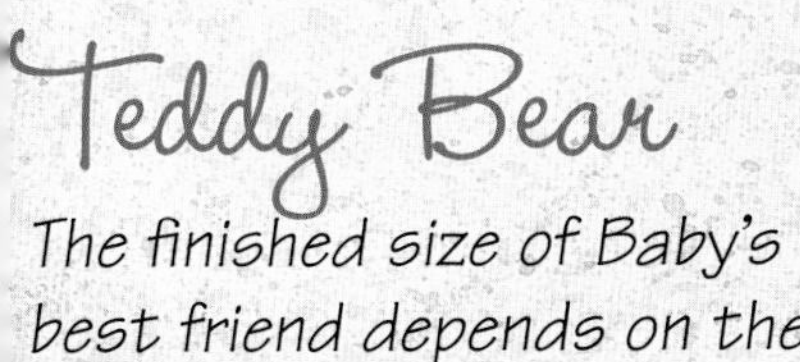

Teddy Bear

The finished size of Baby's best friend depends on the thickness of the yarn you choose.

Instructions on page 27

Felted Purse

EASY

Shown on page 2.

Finished Size After Felting:
11"w x $7^{1}/_{2}$"h x $4^{1}/_{2}$"d
(28 cm x 19 cm x 11.5 cm)

Materials

MEDIUM 4

100% Wool Medium
Weight Yarn (not superwash)
[$3^{1}/_{2}$ ounces, 223 yards
(100 grams, 204 meters)
per skein]:
- Blue - 2 skeins
- Red - 2 skeins
- Teal - 2 skeins
- Green - 2 skeins
- Gold - 2 skeins

2 - 50" (127 cm) lengths of scrap cotton yarn (for felting)
29" (73.5 cm) Circular knitting needle, size 15 (10 mm) **or** size needed for gauge
Double pointed knitting needles, size 15 (10 mm)
Split-ring marker
Suede lace - small amount
Yarn needle

Gauge

Using 2 strands, in Stockinette Stitch,
10 sts and 13 rows = 4" (10 cm)
(before felting)

See Felting Basics, page 34.

Entire purse is worked holding two strands of yarn together.

Body

Bottom

With Blue and circular needle, cast on 32 sts.

Rows 1-25: Knit across.

Sides

Do **not** cut Blue ***(see Changing Colors, page 33)***; with Red, knit across, pick up 18 sts evenly spaced across end of rows ***(Figs. 21a & b, page 33)***, pick up 32 sts evenly spaced across cast on edge, pick up 18 sts evenly spaced across end of rows, place marker ***(see Circular Knitting, page 33 and Markers, page 30)***: 100 sts.

Rnds 1-6: Knit around.

When instructed to slip a stitch, always slip as if to **purl**.

Rnd 7: With Teal, (K1, slip 1) around.

Rnd 8: With Green, (slip 1, K1) around.

Rnds 9 and 10: Knit around.

Rnd 11: With Gold, (slip 1, K1) around.

Rnd 12: With Green, knit around.

Rnd 13: With Gold, knit around.

Rnd 14: With Blue, slip 2, K1, (slip 3, K1) around to last st, slip 1.

Rnd 15: Slip 1, K2, (slip 2, K2) around to last st, slip 1.

Rnds 16 and 17: With Gold, knit around.

Rnd 18: With Teal, (K1, slip 1) around.

Rnd 19: With Gold, knit around.

Rnd 20: With Red, knit around.

Rnd 21: With Green, (K1, slip 3) around.

Rnd 22: K2, slip 1, (K3, slip 1) around to last st, K1.

Rnd 23: With Blue, knit around.

Rnds 24 and 25: With Green, knit around.

Rnd 26: With Gold, (K1, slip 1) around.

Rnds 27 and 28: With Green, knit around.

Rnd 29: With Teal, (slip 1, K3) around.

Rnd 30: With Green, K2, slip 1, (K3, slip 1) around to last st, K1.

Rnd 31: With Teal, (K1, slip 1) around.

Rnds 32 and 33: With Gold, knit around.

Rnd 34: With Blue, slip 1, K1, (slip 3, K1) around to last 2 sts, slip 2.

Rnd 35: With Gold, knit around.

Rnd 36: With Red, slip 2, K1, (slip 3, K1) around to last st, slip 1.

Rnd 37: With Blue, (slip 1, K3) around.

Rnd 38: (K1, slip 1) around.

Rnd 39: With Gold, (slip 1, K1) around.

Rnd 40: Knit around.

Rnd 41: With Green, (K2, slip 2) around.

Rnd 42: With Teal, K1, slip 1, (K3, slip 1) around to last 2 sts, K2.

Rnd 43: Knit around.

Rnd 44: (K 18, K2 tog) around ***(Fig. 9, page 31)***: 95 sts.

Bind off all sts in **knit**.

Straps (Make 2)

First Bobble

Loosely wind four 1¼" (3 cm) diameter balls of Red to be used later to stuff the Bobbles.

Using double pointed needles and Red, and leaving a long end for sewing, cast on 3 sts.

Row 1 (Right side)**:** Knit increase twice ***(Figs. 7a & b, page 31)***, K1: 5 sts.

Row 2: Purl across.

Row 3: Knit increase 4 times, K1: 9 sts.

Row 4: Purl across.

Row 5: Knit increase 8 times, K1: 17 sts.

Row 6: Purl across.

Row 7: Knit across.

Row 8: Purl across.

Row 9: SSK 4 times ***(Figs. 12a-c, page 32)***, K2 tog 4 times, K1: 9 sts.

Row 10: Purl across.

Row 11: K1, SSK, K3, K2 tog, K1: 7 sts.

Center

Row 1: Slide sts to opposite end of needle, K7.

Repeat Row 1 until Center measures approximately 31½" (80 cm) from top of First Bobble.

Second Bobble

Row 1: Knit increase, K4, knit increase, K1: 9 sts.

Row 2: Purl across.

Row 3: Knit increase 8 times, K1: 17 sts.

Row 4: Purl across.

Row 5: Knit across.

Row 6: Purl across.

Row 7: SSK 4 times, K2 tog 4 times, K1: 9 sts.

Row 8: Purl across.

Row 9: SSK twice, K2 tog twice, K1: 5 sts.

Row 10: Purl across.

Row 11: SSK, K2 tog, K1: 3 sts.

Cut yarn leaving a long end for sewing. Thread yarn needle with end and weave through remaining sts, pulling **tightly** to close, then weave ends of rows of Bobble together, ending at base of Bobble and inserting wound ball of yarn before closing.

Thread yarn needle with cast on end and weave through base of cast on row, pulling **tightly** to close. Weave ends of rows of Bobble together, ending at top of Bobble and inserting wound ball of yarn before closing.

To prevent the opening from rippling during felting, weave a length of cotton yarn through last round of Body of purse; weave a second strand of cotton yarn approximately ½" (12 mm) below. Draw up strands slightly and tie in a knot. Felt Body and Straps. Remove cotton yarn. When completely dry, attach Straps to Body using suede lace.

Design by Joan Beebe.

Clutch

EASY

Shown on page 3.

Finished Size After Felting:
5"h x 7"l (12.5 cm x 18 cm)

Materials

MEDIUM 4

100% Wool Medium Weight Yarn (not superwash)
[3 ounces, 158 yards (85 grams, 144 meters) per skein]:
Orange - 1 skein
[2$^3/_4$ ounces, 143 yards (78 grams, 131 meters) per skein]:
Variegated - 1 skein
2 - 20" (51 cm) lengths of scrap cotton yarn (for felting)
Straight knitting needles, size 10 (6 mm) **or** size needed for gauge
24" (61 cm) Circular knitting needle, size 10 (6 mm)
Split-ring markers
2" (5 cm) Button
Exclusively You® Gold tone magnetic clasp, item #28344
Yarn needle

Gauge

In Stockinette Stitch,
17 sts and 20 rows = 4" (10 cm)
(before felting)

See Felting Basics, page 34.

Body

Front

With Orange, cast on 36 sts.

Rows 1-33: Beginning with a **purl** row, work in Stockinette Stitch.

Bind off all sts in **knit**.

Back & Flap

With Orange, cast on 36 sts.

Rows 1-33: Beginning with a **purl** row, work in Stockinette Stitch.

Place a marker in first and last st on last row ***(see Markers, page 30)***.

Rows 34 and 35: Work in Stockinette Stitch.

Row 36 (Decrease row): SSK ***(Figs. 12a-c, page 32)***, knit across to last 2 sts, K2 tog ***(Fig. 9, page 31)***: 34 sts.

Row 37: Purl across.

Rows 38-50: Repeat Rows 36 and 37, 6 times; then repeat Row 36 once **more**: 20 sts.

Row 51 (Decrease row): P2 tog ***(Fig. 15, page 32)***, purl across to last 2 sts, P2 tog: 18 sts.

Row 52 (Decrease row): SSK, knit across to last 2 sts, K2 tog: 16 sts.

Rows 53-57: Repeat Rows 51 and 52 twice, then repeat Row 51 once **more**: 6 sts.

Bind off remaining sts in **knit**.

Finishing

Front Edging

With **knit** side of Front facing, using circular needle and Variegated, and beginning at bound off edge, pick up 24 sts across end of rows ***(Figs. 21a & b, page 33)***, **turn**; add on 2 sts ***(Figs. 20a & b, page 33)***, **turn**; working across cast on edge, pick up one st in base of each st across, **turn**; add on 2 sts, **turn**; pick up 24 sts across end of rows: 88 sts.

Row 1: Knit across.

Bind off all sts in **knit**.

Back & Flap Edging

With Variegated and circular needle, cast on 2 sts.

With **knit** side facing and working across cast on edge, pick up one stitch at base of each st, **turn**; add on 2 sts, **turn**; working in end of rows, pick up 24 sts evenly spaced across to marker, do **not** remove marker, pick up 26 sts evenly spaced across end of rows to bound off edge, pick up one stitch in each st across bound off edge, pick up 26 sts evenly spaced across end of rows to next marker, do **not** remove marker, pick up 24 sts evenly spaced across end of rows, place marker to mark beginning of rnd: 146 sts.

Rnd 1: Purl around.

Bind off all sts in **knit**.

With **purl** sides of Front and Back together, using Variegated and matching bound off sts and beginning at marker, **loosely** sew pieces together, ending at second marker.

To prevent the opening from rippling during felting, weave a length of cotton yarn through last row at top of Front gathering slightly, then weave a second length 1/2" (12 mm) below, gather slightly and secure ends.

Felt Clutch. Remove cotton yarn.

Add magnetic clasp. Sew button to Flap over magnetic clasp.

Textured Purse

EASY

Shown on page 4.

Finished Size: 10"w x 10"l (25.5 cm x 25.5 cm)

Materials

Bulky Weight Yarn (BULKY 5)
- [5 ounces, 153 yards (140 grams, 140 meters) per skein]: 2 skeins

Straight knitting needles, size 10 1/2 (6.5 mm) **or** size needed for gauge

Double pointed knitting needles, size 10 1/2 (6.5 mm)

Split-ring markers

Exclusively You® Large Plastic Brown/Black Rings, item #28371 - 2 packages

Fabric for lining - 1/2 yard (1/2 meter)

1/2" (12 mm) Covered Poly Boning - 5/8 yard (57 cm)

Exclusively You® Gold tone magnetic clasp, item #28344

Sewing needle and thread

Yarn needle

Gauge

In pattern,
14 sts and 18 rows = 4" (10 cm)

Body (Make 2)

Cast on 24 sts.

Row 1: (K1, P1) across.

Row 2 (Right side)**:** Add on 2 sts ***(Figs. 20a & b, page 33)***, (K1, P1) across: 26 sts.

Rows 3 and 4: Add on 2 sts, (P1, K1) across: 30 sts.

Rows 5 and 6: Add on 2 sts, (K1, P1) across: 34 sts.

Row 7: Add on 2 sts, (P1, K1) across: 36 sts.

Row 8: (P1, K1) across.

Rows 9 and 10: (K1, P1) across.

Rows 11 and 12: (P1, K1) across.

Repeat Rows 9-12 for pattern until Body measures approximately 8 3/4" (22 cm) from cast on edge, ending by working Row 12.

Place a marker in first and last st on last row ***(see Markers, page 30)***.

Top Shaping

Row 1: P2 tog tbl ***(Fig. 16, page 32)***, K1, (P1, K1) 6 times, bind off next 8 sts in pattern, (K1, P1) across to last 2 sts, K2 tog ***(Fig. 9, page 31)***: **before** turning work, 14 sts on first side and 12 sts on second side.

Continued on page 16

Both sides of Top Shaping are worked at the same time, using separate yarn for **each** side.

Row 2: (P1, K1) across; with second yarn, bind off 2 sts, K1, (P1, K1) across: 12 sts **each** side.

Row 3: P2 tog tbl, (K1, P1) across; with second yarn, bind off 2 sts, P1, (K1, P1) across to last 2 sts, K2 tog: **before** turning work, 11 sts on first side and 9 sts on second side.

Row 4: P1, (K1, P1) across; with second yarn, bind off 2 sts, (P1, K1) across: 9 sts **each** side.

Row 5: P2 tog tbl, K1, (P1, K1) across; with second yarn, bind off 2 sts, (K1, P1) twice, K2 tog: **before** turning work, 8 sts on first side and 6 sts on second side.

Row 6: (P1, K1) across; with second yarn, bind off 2 sts, K1, (P1, K1) across: 6 sts **each** side.

Strap

Row 1: Bind off 6 sts in **purl**; with **right** side facing, pull working yarn **behind** sts and with double pointed needle, K6.

Row 2: Slide sts to opposite end of needle, with second double pointed needle, K6.

Row 3: Slide sts to opposite end of needle, K6.

Repeat Row 3 until Strap measures approximately 27" (68.5 cm).

Bind off all sts in **knit**.

Weave Strap through first set of rings as follows: Come up through first ring, down through second ring **and** first ring, then up through second ring ***(Photo A)***. Slide rings to beginning end of Strap.

Photo A

Weave Strap through second set of rings as follows: go down through first ring, up through second ring **and** first ring, then down through second ring ***(Photo B)***.

Photo B

Sew end of Strap to 6 bound off sts on last row of opposite side of Body. Slide rings to end of Strap over seam.

Finishing

Using Body as a pattern, cut 2 pieces of fabric 1/4" (7 mm) larger than Body, beginning and ending at markers; then cut lining straight across top, 1/2" (12 mm) above markers.

With **wrong** sides of Body together and beginning at marker, sew pieces together, ending at second marker.

Matching right sides and raw edges and using a 1/2" (12 mm) seam allowance, sew lining along long curved edge. Clip curved edge. Press 1" (2.5 cm) to wrong side along top edge of lining. Cut 2 strips of boning equal to the width of the lining. Remove plastic boning from fabric sleeve. Position sleeve 1/4" (7 mm) below fold line on wrong side of lining and stitch to lining, working over existing stitch lines. Stitch across one end of boning sleeve. Trim 1/4" (7 mm) off plastic boning, reinsert in sleeve and stitch second end closed. Repeat for second side. Using back plate of magnetic clasp as a guide, cut small slits through folded lining for the prongs of the clasp, working **around** plastic boning. Slip prongs through holes in lining and through the back plates. Bend prongs out flat. Insert lining into purse and sew top edge of lining to purse.

Design by Joan Beebe.

Textured Stripes Afghan

EASY

Shown on page 5.

Finished Size:
46"w x 60"l (117 cm x 152.5 cm)

Materials

Medium Weight Yarn [4 MEDIUM]
[6 ounces, 312 yards (170 grams, 285 meters) per skein]:
- Lt Teal - 4 skeins
- Green - 2 skeins

[5 ounces, 260 yards (141 grams, 238 meters) per skein]:
- Dk Teal - 6 skeins

29" (73.5 cm) Circular knitting needle, size 15 (10 mm) **or** size needed for gauge

Gauge

Using 2 strands, in Garter Stitch (knit every row), 9 sts = 4" (10 cm)

Entire Afghan is worked holding two strands of yarn together.

Afghan

With Dk Teal, cast on 103 sts.

Rows 1-6: Knit across.

Cut Dk Teal.

Rows 7 and 8: With Green, knit across.

Cut Green.

Rows 9-11: With Lt Teal, knit across.

Row 12: Purl across; do **not** cut Lt Teal.

Row 13: WYB slip 1 as if to **purl**, ★ with Dk Teal, [K, K tbl ***(Fig. 2, page 30)***, K] **all** in next st, WYB slip 1 as if to **purl**; repeat from ★ across: 205 sts.

Row 14: WYF slip 1 as if to **purl**, ★ K3 tog ***(Fig. 10, page 31)***, WYF slip 1 as if to **purl**; repeat from ★ across; cut Dk Teal: 103 sts.

Row 15: With Lt Teal, knit across.

Row 16: Purl across.

Rows 17 and 18: Knit across.

Cut Lt Teal.

Rows 19 and 20: With Green, knit across.

Cut Green.

Rows 21-23: With Dk Teal, knit across.

Row 24: Purl across; do **not** cut Dk Teal.

Row 25: WYB slip 1 as if to **purl**, ★ with Lt Teal, [K, K tbl, K] **all** in next st, WYB slip 1 as if to **purl**; repeat from ★ across: 205 sts.

Row 26: WYF slip 1 as if to **purl**, ★ K3 tog, WYF slip 1 as if to **purl**; repeat from ★ across; cut Lt Teal: 103 sts.

Row 27: With Dk Teal, knit across.

Row 28: Purl across.

Rows 29 and 30: Knit across.

Cut Dk Teal.

Repeat Rows 7-30 for pattern until afghan measures approximately 58½" (148.5 cm) from cast on edge, ending by working Row 20; cut Green.

Last 6 Rows: With Dark Teal, knit across.

Bind off all sts in **knit**.

Design by Melissa Leapman.

Dog Sweater

EASY

Shown on page 6.

Size	Chest Measurement
X-Small	12" (30.5 cm)
Small	16" (40.5 cm)
Medium	20" (51 cm)
Large	24" (61 cm)
X-Large	28" (71 cm)
XX-Large	32" (81.5 cm)

Size Note: Instructions are written with sizes X-Small, Small, and Medium in first set of braces { }, and sizes Large, X-Large, and XX-Large in second set of braces. Instructions will be easier to read if you circle all the numbers pertaining to the size you are knitting.

Materials

BULKY 5

Bulky Weight Yarn
[3 ounces, 108 yards (85 grams, 99 meters) per skein]: {1-1-2}{2-3-3} skein(s)
Straight knitting needles, size 11 (8 mm) **or** size needed for gauge
1" (2.5 cm) Button
Sewing needle and thread
Yarn needle

Gauge

In K2, P2 ribbing,
12 sts and 13 rows = 3½" (9 cm)

Ribbing

Cast on {22-30-42}{50-58-66} sts.

Work in K1, P1 ribbing for {4-4½-5} {5½-6-6½}"/ {10-11.5-12.5}{14-15-16.5} cm.

Body

Row 1 (Right side)**:** K2, (P2, K2) across.

Row 2: P2, (K2, P2) across.

Repeat Rows 1 and 2 until piece measures approximately {10-12-14}{16-18-20}"/ {25.5-30.5-35.5}{40.5-45.5-51} cm from cast on edge, ending by working Row 2.

Shaping

Rows 1-6: K1, SSK ***(Figs. 12a-c, page 32)***, knit across to last 3 sts, K2 tog ***(Fig. 9, page 31)***, K1: {10-18-30}{38-46-54} sts.

Bind off all sts in **knit**.

Tummy Strap

Cast on {12-18-24}{30-36-42} sts.

Knit {2-2-4}{6-8-8} rows.

Buttonhole Row: K1, YO ***(Fig. 3, page 30)*** **(buttonhole made)**, K2 tog, K2, YO **(buttonhole made)**, K2 tog, knit across.

Knit {2-2-4}{6-8-8} rows.

Bind off all sts in **knit**.

Sew Tummy Strap to right edge of Body beginning {6½-7½-8½}{9½-10½-11½}"/ {16.5-19-21.5}{24-26.5-29} cm from cast on edge.

Weave end of rows of K1, P1 Ribbing together ***(Fig. 22, page 34)***.

Sew button to side of Body opposite buttonhole.

Design by Shelle Hendrix Cain.

Flowered Stole

EASY

Shown on page 7.

Finished Size: 24"w x 70"l (61 cm x 178 cm)

Materials

Medium Weight Yarn
[3½ ounces, 210 yards (100 grams, 192 meters) per skein]:
- Brown - 7 skeins
- Green - 1 skein
- Tan - 1 skein
- Mauve - 1 skein

Straight knitting needles, sizes 7 (4.5 mm) **and** 9 (5.5 mm) **or** sizes needed for gauge
Double pointed knitting needles, size 7 (4.5 mm)
Yarn needle

Gauge

With larger size needles, in pattern, 20 sts and 26 rows = 4" (10 cm)

Stole

With larger size needles and Brown, cast on 120 sts.

Rows 1 and 2: K1, (P1, K1) across to last st, WYF slip 1 as if to **purl**.

Rows 3 and 4: K2, P1, (K1, P1) across to last st, WYF slip 1 as if to **purl**.

Repeat Rows 1-4 for pattern until Stole measures approximately 70" (178 cm) from cast on edge, ending by working Row 1 or Row 3.

Bind off all sts in pattern.

Vine

With Green and double pointed needles, cast on 3 sts.

Row 1: Slide sts to opposite end of needle, K3.

Repeat Row 1 until Vine measures approximately 4 yards (3.5 meters).

Bind off all sts in **knit**.

Small Flower (Make 3)

With smaller size straight needles and Tan, cast on 62 sts.

Row 1: Purl across.

Row 2 (Right side)**:** K3, slip last st back onto left needle (base st), pass the next 8 sts over the base st, † give the working yarn a slight tug to tighten up the petal, YO twice ***(Fig. A)***, knit the base st again, K3, slip last st back onto left needle (base st) †, pass the next 12 sts over the base st, repeat from † to † once, pass the next 8 sts over the base st, repeat from † to † once, pass the next 10 sts over the base st, repeat from † to † once, pass the next 7 sts over the base st, give the working yarn a slight tug to tighten up the petal, YO twice, knit the base st again, K2: 27 sts.

Fig. A

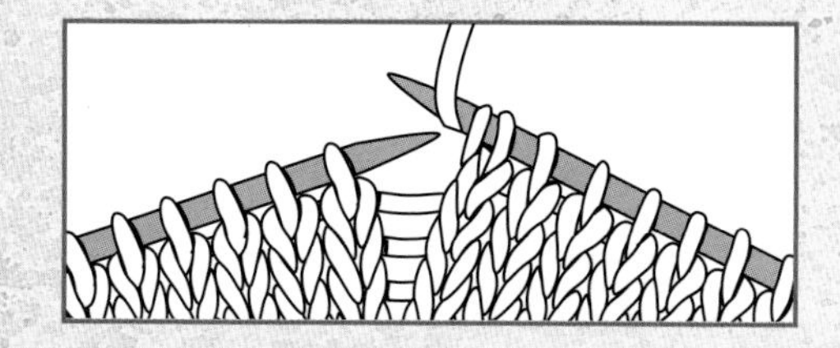

Row 3: ★ P1, P2 tog ***(Fig. 15, page 32)***, purl into the **front** of the first YO, purl into the **back** of the second YO; repeat from ★ across to last 2 sts, P2: 22 sts.

Row 4: P2 tog across: 11 sts.

Cut yarn; thread yarn needle with end and weave through remaining sts, pulling **tightly** to close. With same end, sew end of rows of first and last petals together.

Center Bobble

With smaller size straight needles and Lavender, leaving a 10" (25.5 cm) end at beginning, cast on 3 sts.

Row 1 (Right side)**:** Knit across.

Continued on page 20

Row 2: Purl increase ***(Fig. 8, page 31)***, P2: 4 sts.

Row 3: Knit increase ***(Figs. 7a & b, page 31)***, K3: 5 sts.

Row 4: Purl increase, P4: 6 sts.

Row 5: Knit across.

Row 6: Purl across.

Row 7: SSK ***(Figs. 12a-c, page 32)***, K4: 5 sts.

Row 8: P2 tog, P3: 4 sts.

Row 9: SSK, K2: 3 sts.

Cut yarn leaving a long end. Wind beginning end into a small ball. Thread needle with long end and weave through remaining sts and around edge of Bobble, pulling **tightly** to close around beginning end. With same end, sew Bobble to center of Small Flower.

Small Leaf (Make 11)

With smaller size straight needles and Green, cast on 3 sts.

Row 1 (Right side): K1, [YO ***(Fig. 3, page 30)***, K1] twice: 5 sts.

Row 2: Purl across.

Row 3: K2, YO, K1, YO, K2: 7 sts.

Row 4: Purl across.

Row 5: K3, YO, K1, YO, K3: 9 sts.

Row 6: Purl across.

Row 7: Knit across.

Rows 8-10: Repeat Rows 6 and 7 once, then repeat Row 6 once **more**.

Row 11: K3, [slip 2 sts together as if to **knit**, K1, P2SSO ***(Figs. 14a & b, page 32)***], K3: 7 sts.

Row 12: Purl across.

Row 13: K2, slip 2 sts together as if to **knit**, K1, P2SSO, K2: 5 sts.

Row 14: Purl across.

Row 15: K1, slip 2 sts together as if to **knit**, K1, P2SSO, K1: 3 sts.

Row 16: Purl across.

Row 17: Slip 2 sts together as if to **knit**, K1, P2SSO; cut yarn leaving a long end for sewing to Stole; pull yarn through last st.

Large Leaf (Make 2)

With smaller size straight needles and Green, cast on 3 sts.

Row 1 (Right side): Knit increase twice, K1: 5 sts.

Row 2 AND ALL WRONG SIDE ROWS: Purl across.

Row 3: Knit increase, K2, knit increase, K1: 7 sts.

Row 5: Knit increase, K4, knit increase, K1: 9 sts.

Rows 7-12: Work in Stockinette Stitch.

Row 13: SSK, K5, K2 tog ***(Fig. 9, page 31)***: 7 sts.

Row 15: SSK, K3, K2 tog: 5 sts.

Row 17: SSK, K1, K2 tog: 3 sts.

Row 19: Slip 2 sts together as if to **knit**, K1, P2SSO; cut yarn leaving a long end for sewing to Stole; pull yarn through last st.

Bud (Make 4)

With Mauve, cast on 5 sts.

Row 1: Purl across.

Row 2 (Right side): ★ † [K, (YO, K) twice] **all** in first st, (**turn**; P5, **turn**; K5) twice, pass second, third, fourth, and fifth sts over first st **(bobble made)** †, K1, pass second st on right needle over first st, slip st back onto left needle; repeat from ★ 3 times **more**, then repeat from † to † once, insert right needle into base of first bobble and pull up a st, pass second st on right needle over first st; cut yarn and pull through last st.

Large Flower (Make 2)

Center

With smaller size straight needles and Mauve, make a slip knot on needle.

Row 1 (Right side): ★ Add on 4 sts ***(Figs. 20a & b, page 33)***, bind off 4 sts **(spike made)**, slip st back to left needle; repeat from ★ 4 times **more**, add on one st: 5 spikes and 2 sts.

Petals

Row 1: K1, knit increase: 3 sts.

Row 2: Knit across.

Row 3: K2, knit increase: 4 sts.

Row 4: Knit across.

Row 5: K3, knit increase: 5 sts.

Rows 6-9: Knit across.

Row 10: Bind off one st, knit across: 4 sts.

Row 11: Knit across.

Rows 12-15: Repeat Rows 10 and 11, twice: 2 sts.

Row 16: Bind off one st, with **right** side facing, insert right needle in sp between first and second spikes of center and pull up a st, pass second st on right needle over first st **(petal joined)**, slip st back to left needle, add on one st: 2 sts.

Rows 17-31: Repeat Rows 1-15.

Row 32: Bind off one st, with **right** side facing, pick up one st in sp between next 2 spikes of center, pass second st on right needle over first st **(petal joined)**.

Rows 33-79: Repeat Rows 17-32 twice, then repeat Rows 17-31 once **more**.

Row 80: Bind off one st, with **right** side facing and working **behind** spikes, insert right needle through base of last spike **and** through base of first spike and pull up a st, pass second st on right needle over first st **(petal joined)**; cut yarn and pull through last st.

Thread needle with end and weave through base on each spike, pulling **tightly** to close center of Flower.

Using photo as a guide for placement, sew Vine, Flowers, Buds and Leaves to Stole.

Design by Joan Beebe.

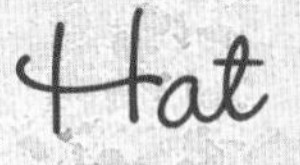

Hat

EASY

Shown on page 8.

Size	Finished Size
Child Small	16½" (42 cm)
Child Medium	18" (45.5 cm)
Child Large	19½" (49.5 cm)
Adult Small	21" (53.5 cm)
Adult Medium	22½" (57 cm)
Adult Large	24" (61 cm)

Size Note: Instructions are written with Child sizes Small, Medium, and Large in first set of braces { } and Adult sizes Small, Medium, and Large in second set of braces. Instructions will be easier to read if you circle all the numbers pertaining to the size you are knitting.

Materials

Bulky Weight Yarn
[3½ ounces, 164 yards (100 grams, 150 meters) per skein]: {1-1-1}{2-2-2} skein(s)
Medium Weight Yarn: small amount
Straight knitting needles, sizes 8 (5 mm) **and** 10½ (6.5 mm) **or** sizes needed for gauge
Markers
Yarn needle

Gauge

With larger size needles and Bulky Weight Yarn, 16 sts and 20 rows = 4" (10 cm) in K1, P1 ribbing.

Body

With larger size needles and Bulky Weight Yarn, cast on {60-66-72}{78-84-90} sts.

Work in K1, P1 ribbing for {7-8-9}{10-11-12}"/{18-20.5-23}{25.5-28-30.5} cm.

Top Shaping

Row 1 (Right side): K{8-9-10}{11-12-13}, K2 tog ***(Fig. 9, page 31)***, ★ place marker ***(see Markers, page 30)***, K{8-9-10}{11-12-13}, K2 tog; repeat from ★ across: {54-60-66}{72-78-84} sts.

Row 2: Purl across.

Row 3 (Decrease row): ★ Knit across to within 2 sts of marker, K2 tog, slip marker; repeat from ★ 4 times **more**, knit across to last 2 sts, K2 tog: {48-54-60}{66-72-78} sts.

Repeat Rows 2 and 3, {6-7-8}{9-10-11} times: 12 sts.

Cut yarn leaving a long end. Thread yarn needle with end and weave through remaining sts, pulling **tightly** to close; weave seam ***(Fig. 22, page 34)***.

With smaller size needles and Medium Weight Yarn, make Small Flower ***(see Flowered Stole Small Flower, page 19)***.

Sew Flower to Hat.

Mittens

INTERMEDIATE

Shown on page 8.

	Child Size		
	Small	**Medium**	**Large**
Width Around Palm	4 1/2" (11.5 cm)	5 1/4" (13.5 cm)	6 1/4" (16 cm)
Hand Length	3 1/2" (9 cm)	4 1/2" (11.5 cm)	5" (12.5 cm)
Thumb Length	1" (2.5 cm)	1 1/2" (4 cm)	2" (5 cm)

	Adult Size		
	Small	**Medium**	**Large**
Width Around Palm	6 3/4" (17 cm)	7 1/2" (19 cm)	8 1/2" (21.5 cm)
Hand Length	6" (15 cm)	6 1/2" (16.5 cm)	7" (18 cm)
Thumb Length	2 1/4" (5.5 cm)	2 1/2" (6.5 cm)	2 3/4" (7 cm)

Size Note: Instructions are written with Child sizes Small, Medium, and Large in the first set of braces { } and Adult sizes Small, Medium, and Large in the second set of braces. Instructions will be easier to read if you circle all the numbers pertaining to the size you are knitting.

Materials

Medium Weight Yarn (MEDIUM 4)
[4 ounces, 192 yards (113 grams, 175 meters) per skein]: 1 skein
Straight knitting needles, sizes 6 (4 mm) **and** 8 (5 mm) **or** sizes needed for gauge
Stitch holders - 2
Markers
Yarn needle

Gauge

With larger size needles, in Stockinette Stitch (knit one row, purl one row), 18 sts and 24 rows = 4" (10 cm)

Right Mitten

Cuff

With smaller size needles, cast on {22-26-30}{32-36-40} sts.

Work in K1, P1 ribbing for {1 1/2-2-2}{3-3-3}"/ {4-5-5}{7.5-7.5-7.5} cm.

Hand

Change to larger size needles.

Beginning with a **knit** row, work {2-2-4}{4-6-6} rows in Stockinette Stitch.

Thumb Gusset

Row 1 (Right side)**:** K{12-14-16}{16-18-20}, place marker ***(see Markers, page 30)***, work right invisible increase ***(Fig. 6, page 31)***, K1, work left invisible increase ***(Figs. 5a & b, page 31)***, place marker, knit across: {24-28-32}{34-38-42} sts.

Row 2: Purl across.

Row 3 (Increase row)**:** Knit across to marker, slip marker, work right invisible increase, knit across to marker, work left invisible increase, slip marker, knit across: {26-30-34}{36-40-44} sts.

Row 4: Purl across.

Repeat Rows 3 and 4, {1-1-2}{3-4-5} times: {28-32-38}{42-48-54} sts.

Thumb

Dividing Row: Knit across to marker and slip sts just worked onto st holder, remove marker, knit across to marker, remove marker, work left invisible increase, slip remaining sts onto second st holder: {8-8-10}{12-14-16} sts.

Work even until Thumb measures approximately {1-1 1/2-2}{2 1/4-2 1/2-2 3/4}"/ {2.5-4-5}{5.5-6.5-7} cm, ending by working a **purl** row.

Decrease Row: K2 tog across ***(Fig 9, page 31)***: {4-4-5}{6-7-8} sts.

Cut yarn leaving a long end. Thread yarn needle with end and weave through remaining sts, pulling **tightly** to close; weave seam ***(Fig. 22, page 34)***.

Top

Row 1: With **right** side facing, slip sts from first st holder onto needle, slip sts from second st holder onto second needle, M1 ***(Figs. 4a & b, page 30)***, knit across: {22-26-30}{32-36-40} sts.

Row 2: Purl across.

Work even until Mitten measures approximately {5-6½-7}{9-9½-10}"/{12.5-16.5-18}{23-24-25.5} cm from cast on edge, ending by working a **purl** row.

Top Shaping

Row 1: K1, [slip 1 as if to **knit**, K1, PSSO ***(Fig. 11, page 32)***], K{6-8-10}{11-13-15}, K2 tog, K1, slip 1 as if to **knit**, K1, PSSO, K{5-7-9}{10-12-14}, K2 tog, K1: {18-22-26}{28-32-36} sts.

Row 2: P1, P2 tog ***(Fig. 15, page 32)***, P{3-5-7}{8-10-12}, P2 tog tbl ***(Fig. 16, page 32)***, P1, P2 tog, P{4-6-8}{9-11-13}, P2 tog tbl, P1: {14-18-22}{24-28-32} sts.

Row 3: K1, slip 1 as if to **knit**, K1, PSSO, K{2-4-6}{7-9-11}, K2 tog, K1, slip 1 as if to **knit**, K1, PSSO, K{1-3-5}{6-8-10}, K2 tog, K1: {10-14-18}{20-24-28} sts.

Child Sizes Medium and Large and Adult Sizes Small, Medium, and Large ONLY
Row 4: P1, P2 tog, P{1-3}{4-6-8}, P2 tog tbl, P1, P2 tog, P{2-4}{5-7-9}, P2 tog tbl, P1: {10-14}{16-20-24} sts.

Child Size Large and Adult Sizes Small, Medium, and Large ONLY
Row 5: K1, slip 1 as if to **knit**, K1, PSSO, K{2}{3-5-7}, K2 tog, K1, slip 1 as if to **knit**, K1, PSSO, K{1}{2-4-6}, K2 tog, K1: {10}{12-16-20} sts.

Adult Sizes Small, Medium, and Large ONLY
Row 6: P1, P2 tog, P{0-2-4} ***(see Zeros, page 30)***, P2 tog tbl, P1, P2 tog, P{1-3-5}, P2 tog tbl, P1: {8-12-16} sts.

Adult Sizes Medium and Large ONLY
Row 7: K1, slip 1 as if to **knit**, K1, PSSO, K{1-3}, K2 tog, K1, slip 1 as if to **knit**, K1, PSSO, K{0-2}, K2 tog, K1: {8-12} sts.

Adult Size Large ONLY
Row 8: P1, P2 tog, P2 tog tbl, P1, P2 tog, P1, P2 tog tbl, P1: 8 sts.

All Sizes
Cut yarn leaving a long end. Thread yarn needle with end and weave through remaining sts, pulling **tightly** to close; weave seam.

Left Mitten

Work same as Right Mitten to Thumb Gusset.

Row 1: K{9-11-13}{15-17-19}, place marker, work right invisible increase, K1, work left invisible increase, place marker, knit across: {24-28-32}{34-38-42} sts.

Complete same as Right Mitten, beginning with Row 2 of Thumb Gusset.

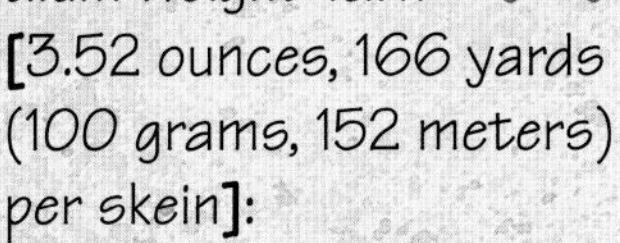

Toe Up Socks

INTERMEDIATE

Shown on page 9.

Finished Ankle Circumference: 7¼{8-9}"/18.5{20.5-23} cm

Size Note: Instructions are written for 7¼" circumference, with 8" and 9" circumferences in braces { }. Instructions will be easier to read if you circle all the numbers pertaining to the size you are knitting. If only one number is given, it applies to all sizes.

Materials

MEDIUM 4

Medium Weight Yarn [3.52 ounces, 166 yards (100 grams, 152 meters) per skein]:
- Green - 1 skein
- Purple - 1 skein

Double pointed knitting needles (set of 5), size 7 (4.5 mm) **or** size needed for gauge
Split-ring markers - 2
Yarn needle

Continued on page 24

Gauge

In Stockinette Stitch,
20 sts and 28 rows = 4" (10 cm)

Toe

With Green, cast on 4 sts.

Beginning with a **knit** row, work 9 rows in Stockinette Stitch.

Toe Shaping

See Using Double Pointed Needles, page 33.

Rnd 1 (Right side)**:** With second needle pick up 6 sts across edge of Toe ***(Figs. 21a & b, page 33)***, with third needle pick up 4 sts across cast on edge, with fourth needle pick up 6 sts across edge of Toe, K2 from first needle; place split-ring marker around next st to mark beginning of rnd ***(see Markers, page 30)***: 20 sts.

Redistribute the sts so there are 5 sts on each of the 4 needles.

Rnd 2: K 10, place second marker around next stitch, knit around.

Rnd 3: Knit around.

Rnd 4 (Increase rnd)**:** K1, M1 ***(Figs. 4a & b, page 30)***, knit across to within one st of next marker, M1, K2, M1, knit across to within one st of next marker, M1, K1: 24 sts.

Rnds 5 thru 10{12-14}: Repeat Rnds 3 and 4, 3{4-5} times: 36{40-44} sts.

Foot

Knit around until piece measures 4" (10 cm) **less** than total desired length from Toe.

Gusset

Rnd 1: Knit across to marker, K1, M1, knit across to within one st of next marker, M1, K1: 38{42-46} sts.

Rnd 2: Knit around.

Rnds 3-16: Repeat Rnds 1 and 2, 7 times: 52{56-60} sts.

Rnds 17-19: Knit around.

Turn Heel

You will be working in rows on double pointed needles to turn and form the Heel

Knit across sts on first and second needle, K 12{13-14} sts on third needle, slip remaining 5 sts onto fourth needle, remove markers.

Row 1: K8, K2 tog ***(Fig. 9, page 31)***, **turn**.

Row 2: P7, P2 tog ***(Fig. 15, page 32)***, **turn**.

Row 3: K6, K2 tog, **turn**.

Row 4: P5, P2 tog, **turn**.

Row 5: K4, K2 tog, **turn**.

Row 6: P3, P2 tog, **turn**.

Row 7: K2, K2 tog, **turn**.

Row 8: P1, P2 tog, **turn**.

Heel

Foundation Rnd: K2, pick up 7 sts along Heel Turning, K 42{46-50}, pick up 7 sts along Heel Turning: 58{62-66} sts.

Row 1: K8, **turn**, leave remaining sts unworked.

Row 2 (Decrease row)**:** Slip 1 as if to **purl**, P 13, P2 tog, **turn**.

Row 3 (Decrease row)**:** (Slip 1 as if to **purl**, K1) 7 times, SSK ***(Figs. 12a-c, page 32)***, **turn**.

Rows 4-22: Repeat Rows 2 and 3, 9 times; then repeat Row 2 once **more**.

Row 23: (Slip 1 as if to **purl**, K1) 7 times, SSK: 36{40-44} sts.

Cuff

Rnd 1: K2{3-4}, knit across sts on next two needles, K9{10-11} sts onto next needle, knit remaining sts onto last needle; place split-ring marker to mark beginning of rnd: 9{10-11} sts on each needle.

Rnds 2-6: Knit around.

Rnd 7: Purl around.

Cut Green.

Rnds 8-11: With Purple, knit around.

Rnd 12 (Turning rnd)**:** ★ K2 tog, YO ***(Fig. 3, page 30)***; repeat from ★ around.

Rnds 13 and 14: Knit around.

Bind off all sts loosely in **knit**.

Fold Cuff to **wrong** side at turning round and sew **loosely** in place.

Design by Lois J. Long.

Blue Booties

INTERMEDIATE

Shown on page 10.

Finished Size: Newborn to 3 months

Materials

Light Weight Yarn (LIGHT 3)
approximately 55 yards (50.5 meters)
Straight knitting needles, size 5 (3.75 mm) **or** size needed for gauge
Stitch holders - 3
Yarn needle
1/4" (7 mm) w Ribbon - 1 yard (1 meter)

Gauge

In Stockinette Stitch (knit one row, purl one row), 12 sts = 2" (5 cm)

Cuff

Cast on 29 sts.

Row 1 (Right side)**:** K2, [work Right Twist ***(Fig. 1, page 30)***, K1] across.

Row 2: (K1, P2) across to last 2 sts, K2.

Row 3: Knit across.

Row 4: (K1, P2) across to last 2 sts, K2.

Rows 5-18: Repeat Rows 1-4, 3 times; then repeat Rows 1 and 2 once **more**.

Row 19: Knit across.

Row 20: Purl across.

Row 21 (Eyelet row)**:** K1, ★ YO ***(Fig. 3, page 30)***, K2 tog ***(Fig. 9, page 31)***; repeat from ★ across.

Row 22: Purl across.

Instep

Row 1: K 10, slip sts just worked onto st holder, K9, slip last 10 sts onto second st holder: 9 sts.

Rows 2-18: Work in Stockinette Stitch for 17 rows.

Slip sts onto third st holder; cut yarn.

Sides

Row 1: With **right** side facing, slip 10 sts from first st holder onto empty needle, pick up 9 sts evenly spaced along right side of Instep ***(Fig. 21a, page 33)***, slip 9 sts from st holder onto empty needle and knit across, pick up 9 sts evenly spaced across left side of Instep, slip 10 sts from last st holder onto empty needle and knit across: 47 sts.

Row 2: (K1, P2) across to last 2 sts, K2.

Row 3: K2, (work Right Twist, K1) across.

Row 4: (K1, P2) across to last 2 sts, K2.

Row 5: Knit across.

Rows 6-11: Repeat Rows 2-5 once, then repeat Rows 2 and 3 once **more**.

Sole

Row 1: P2 tog tbl ***(Fig. 16, page 32)***, P 19, P2 tog tbl, P1, P2 tog ***(Fig. 15, page 32)***, P 19, P2 tog: 43 sts.

Row 2: Knit across.

Row 3: P2 tog tbl, P 17, P2 tog tbl, P1, P2 tog, P 17, P2 tog: 39 sts.

Bind off all sts in **knit**.

Finishing

Sew Sole and back in one continuous seam.

Weave an 18" (45.5 cm) length of ribbon through Eyelet row.

Design by Joan Beebe.

Pink Booties

INTERMEDIATE

Shown on page 10.

Finished Size: Newborn to 3 months

Materials

Light Weight Yarn: LIGHT 3
approximately 55 yards (50.5 meters)
Straight knitting needles, size 5 (3.75 mm) **or** size needed for gauge
Stitch holders - 3
Yarn needle
1/4" (7 mm) w Ribbon - 1 yard (1 meter)

Gauge

In Stockinette Stitch,
12 sts = 2" (5 cm)

Cuff

Cast on 31 sts.

Row 1: Purl across.

Row 2 (Right side)**:** Knit across.

Row 3: Purl across.

Row 4 (Picot ridge)**:** K1, ★ YO ***(Fig. 3, page 30)***, K2 tog ***(Fig. 9, page 31)***; repeat from ★ across.

Rows 5-8: Repeat Rows 1 and 2 twice.

Row 9: Purl across to last st, purl increase ***(Fig. 8, page 31)***: 32 sts.

Row 10: K4, YO, [slip 1 as if to **knit**, K2 tog, PSSO ***(Figs. 13a & b, page 32)***], YO, ★ K3, YO, slip 1 as if to **knit**, K2 tog, PSSO, YO; repeat from ★ 3 times **more**, K1.

Row 11: Purl across.

Row 12: K1, YO, slip 1 as if to **knit**, K2 tog, PSSO, YO, ★ K3, YO, slip 1 as if to **knit**, K2 tog, PSSO, YO; repeat from ★ 3 times **more**, K4.

Row 13: Purl across.

Rows 14-21: Repeat Rows 10-13 twice.

Row 22: K7, [slip 1 as if to **knit**, K1, PSSO ***(Fig. 11, page 32)***], (K6, K2 tog) twice, K7: 29 sts.

Row 23: Purl across.

Row 24 (Eyelet row)**:** K1, (YO, K2 tog) across.

Row 25: Purl across.

Instep

Row 1: K 10, slip sts just worked onto st holder, K9, slip last 10 sts onto second st holder: 9 sts.

Rows 2-18: Work in Stockinette Stitch for 17 rows.

Slip sts onto third st holder; cut yarn.

Sides

Row 1: With **right** side facing, slip 10 sts from first st holder onto empty needle, pick up 9 sts evenly spaced along right side of Instep ***(Fig. 21a, page 33)***, slip 9 sts from st holder onto empty needle and knit across, pick up 9 sts evenly spaced across left side of Instep, slip 10 sts from last st holder onto empty needle and knit across: 47 sts.

Rows 2-10: Work in Stockinette Stitch for 9 rows.

Sole

Row 1 (Right side)**:** P2 tog ***(Fig. 15, page 32)***, P 19, P2 tog, P1, P2 tog, P 19, P2 tog: 43 sts.

Row 2: Knit across.

Row 3: P2 tog, P 17, P2 tog, P1, P2 tog, P 17, P2 tog: 39 sts.

Bind off all sts in **knit**.

Finishing

Sew Sole and back in one continuous seam.

Fold cast on edge of Cuff to inside along Picot ridge; sew hem **loosely**.

Weave an 18" (45.5 cm) length of ribbon through Eyelet row.

Design by Barbara Botello.

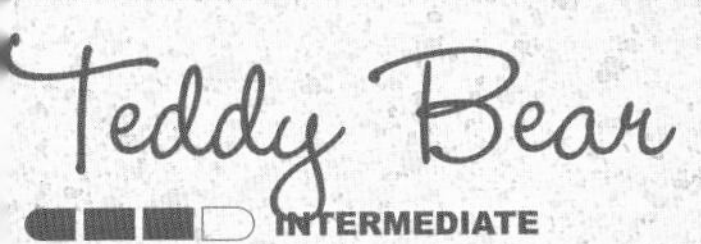

Shown on page 11.

Finished Size: Size will vary depending on the yarn and gauge you choose.

Materials

Yarn of your choice
Straight knitting needles, 1-2 sizes **smaller** than the size recommended on the yarn label. For our models, Bulky Weight Yarn produced a 9" (23 cm) Bear; Light Weight Yarn produced a 7" (18 cm) Bear
Polyester fiberfill
Felt scrap
Floss
Yarn needle
Soft Sculpture needle
Embroidery needle

Gauge

We recommend working to a gauge that is tighter than the gauge recommended for the yarn so that the Bear's stuffing will not be visible.

Body

Cast on 26 sts.

Row 1: Purl across.

Row 2 (Right side)**:** K6, M1 ***(Figs. 4a & b, page 30)***, K2, M1, K 10, M1, K2, M1, K6: 30 sts.

Row 3: Purl across.

Row 4: K7, M1, K2, M1, K 12, M1, K2, M1, K7: 34 sts.

Rows 5-13: Beginning with a **purl** row, work in Stockinette Stitch (purl one row, knit one row).

Row 14: K6, K2 tog ***(Fig. 9, page 31)***, K2, SSK ***(Figs. 12a-c, page 32)***, K 10, K2 tog, K2, SSK, K6: 30 sts.

Row 15: Purl across.

Row 16: K5, K2 tog, K2, SSK, K8, K2 tog, K2, SSK, K5: 26 sts.

Row 17: Purl across.

Row 18: K4, K2 tog, K2, SSK, K6, K2 tog, K2, SSK, K4: 22 sts.

Row 19 (Neck)**:** Purl across.

Row 20: K5, M1, K2, M1, (K3, M1, K2, M1) twice, K5: 28 sts.

Row 21: Purl across.

Row 22: K 11, M1, K6, M1, K 11: 30 sts.

Rows 23-27: Beginning with a **purl** row, work in Stockinette Stitch.

Row 28: K4, (SSK, K2, K2 tog, K2) twice, K2 tog, K2, SSK, K4: 24 sts.

Row 29: Purl across.

Row 30: K4, SSK, K2 tog, (K2, SSK, K2 tog) twice, K4: 18 sts.

Row 31: Purl across.

Bind off all sts in **knit**.

Weave back seam ***(Fig. 22, page 34)***.

Stuff Body, then flatten with seam at center back. Sew top and bottom seams.

Arm (Make 2)

Cast on 11 sts.

Rows 1-5: Beginning with a **purl** row, work in Stockinette Stitch.

Row 6 (Right side)**:** K1, M1, K9, M1, K1: 13 sts.

Rows 7-13: Beginning with a **purl** row, work in Stockinette Stitch.

Row 14: K1, (K2 tog, K1) across: 9 sts.

Row 15: P1, P2 tog across ***(Fig. 15, page 32)***: 5 sts.

Cut yarn leaving a long end. Thread yarn needle with end and weave through remaining sts, pulling **tightly** to close. With same end, weave seam to cast on edge. Stuff Arm, then flatten with seam at back. Sew top seam.

Continued on page 28

Leg (Make 2)
Cast on 11 sts.

Rows 1-3: Beginning with a **purl** row, work in Stockinette Stitch.

Row 4 (Right side)**:** K1, M1, K9, M1, K1: 13 sts.

Rows 5-11: Beginning with a **purl** row, work in Stockinette Stitch.

Row 12: K5, M1, K3, M1, K5: 15 sts.

Row 13: Purl across.

Row 14: K4, SSK, K3, K2 tog, K4: 13 sts.

Row 15: Purl across.

Row 16: K1, (K2 tog, K1) across: 9 sts.

Row 17: P1, P2 tog across: 5 sts.

Cut yarn leaving a long end. Thread yarn needle with end and weave through remaining sts, pulling **tightly** to close. With same end, weave seam to cast on edge. Stuff Leg, then flatten with seam at back. Sew top seam.

Ear (Make 2)
Cast on 12 sts.

Row 1: Purl across.

Row 2 (Right side)**:** K2 tog across: 6 sts.

Row 3: P2 tog across: 3 sts.

Row 4: K3 tog ***(Fig. 10, page 31)***; cut yarn and pull through last st.

Finishing
Sew Ears to Head.

Cut 8 circular disks from scrap of felt.

To attach Arms, thread soft sculpture needle with doubled 24" (61 cm) length of floss. Place one disk on each side of Arm. Insert needle through felt disk and Arm ***(Fig. B)***, then through second felt disk; insert needle back through second felt disk and Arm (at 2), then through first felt disk again (at 1). Insert needle completely through Body and out second side (at 3), through third felt disk and second Arm, then through fourth felt disk (at 4); insert needle back through fourth felt disk, Arm, and third felt disk, and back through Body. Repeat sequence, creating an X pattern on the outer felt disks.

Attach Legs in same manner.

Fig. B

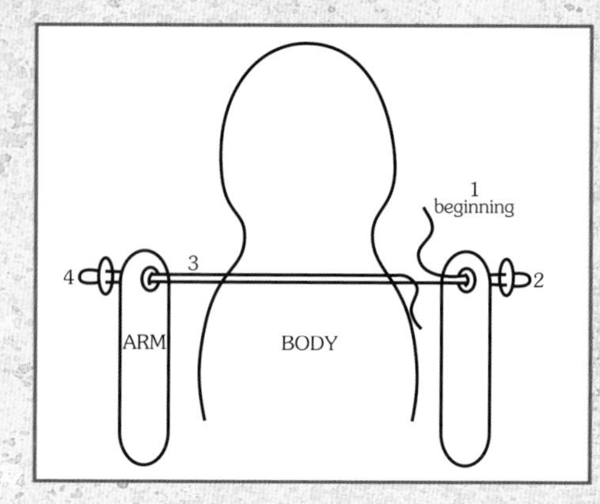

With yarn and additional felt, and using photo as a guide, add facial features ***(see Embroidery Stitches, page 34)***.

Add bow.

Design by Joan Beebe.

General Instructions

Abbreviations

cm centimeters
K knit
M1 make one
mm millimeters
P purl
PSSO pass slipped stitch over
P2SSO pass 2 slipped stitches over
Rnd(s) Round(s)
SSK slip, slip, knit
st(s) stitch(es)
tbl through back loop
tog together
WYB with yarn in back
WYF with yarn in front
YO yarn over

★ — work instructions following ★ as many **more** times as indicated in addition to the first time.

† to † — work all instructions from first † to second † **as many** times as specified.

( ) or [ ] — work enclosed instructions **as many** times as specified by the number immediately following **or** work all enclosed instructions in the stitch or space indicated **or** contains explanatory remarks.

colon (:) — the number(s) given after a colon at the end of a row or round denote(s) the number of stitches or spaces you should have on that row or round.

work even — work without increasing or decreasing in the established pattern.

KNIT TERMINOLOGY		
UNITED STATES		**INTERNATIONAL**
gauge	=	tension
bind off	=	cast off
yarn over (YO)	=	yarn forward (yfwd) **or** yarn around needle (yrn)

Yarn Weight Symbol & Names	LACE 0	SUPER FINE 1	FINE 2	LIGHT 3	MEDIU 4	BULKY 5	SUPER BULKY 6
Type of Yarns in Category	Fingering, size 10 crochet thread	Sock, Fingering, Baby	Sport, Baby	DK, Light Worsted	Worsted, Afghan, Aran	Chunky, Craft, Rug	Bulky, Roving
Knit Gauge Range* in Stockinette St to 4" (10 cm)	33-40** sts	27-32 sts	23-26 sts	21-24 sts	16-20 sts	12-15 sts	6-11 sts
Advised Needle Size Range	000-1	1 to 3	3 to 5	5 to 7	7 to 9	9 to 11	11 and larger

*GUIDELINES ONLY: The chart above reflects the most commonly used gauges and needle sizes for specific yarn categories.

** Lace weight yarns are usually knitted on larger needles to create lacy openwork patterns. Accordingly, a gauge range is difficult to determine. Always follow the gauge stated in your pattern.

KNITTING NEEDLES																
U.S.	0	1	2	3	4	5	6	7	8	9	10	10½	11	13	15	17
U.K.	13	12	11	10	9	8	7	6	5	4	3	2	1	00	000	---
Metric - mm	2	2.25	2.75	3.25	3.5	3.75	4	4.5	5	5.5	6	6.5	8	9	10	12.75

BEGINNER	Projects for first-time knitters using basic knit and purl stitches. Minimal shaping.
EASY	Projects using basic stitches, repetitive stitch patterns, simple color changes, and simple shaping and finishing.
INTERMEDIATE	Projects with a variety of stitches, such as basic cables and lace, simple intarsia, double-pointed needles and knitting in the round needle techniques, mid-level shaping and finishing.
EXPERIENCED	Projects using advanced techniques and stitches, such as short rows, fair isle, more intricate intarsia, cables, lace patterns, and numerous color changes.

Gauge

Exact gauge is **essential** for proper size or fit. Before beginning your project, make a swatch in the yarn and needle specified. After completing the swatch, measure it, counting your stitches and rows carefully. If you have more or less stitches per inch than specified, **make another, changing needle size to get the correct gauge**. Keep trying until you find the size needles that will give you the specified gauge.

Markers

As a convenience to you, we have used markers to help distinguish the beginning of a pattern or round. Place markers as instructed. When using double pointed needles and marking the beginning of a round, a split-ring marker is placed around the first stitch to prevent the marker from slipping off the needle. When you reach the marker, move it to the new stitch after it has been made. When marking placement for decreases or using circular or straight needles, you may use markers or tie a length of contrasting color yarn around the needle. When you reach a marker, slip it from the left needle to the right needle; remove it when instructed or when no longer needed.

Zeros

To consolidate the length of an involved pattern, zeros are sometimes used so that all sizes can be combined. For example, increase every sixth row 5{1-0} time(s) means the first size would increase 5 times, the second size would increase once, and the largest size would do nothing.

Right Twist

(abbreviated RT)

(uses 2 sts)

Insert the right needle into the **front** of the first two stitches on the left needle as if to **knit *(Fig. 9, page 31)***, then **knit** them together as if they were one stitch, making sure not to drop off, then knit the first stitch ***(Fig. 1)*** letting both sts drop off needle together.

Fig. 1

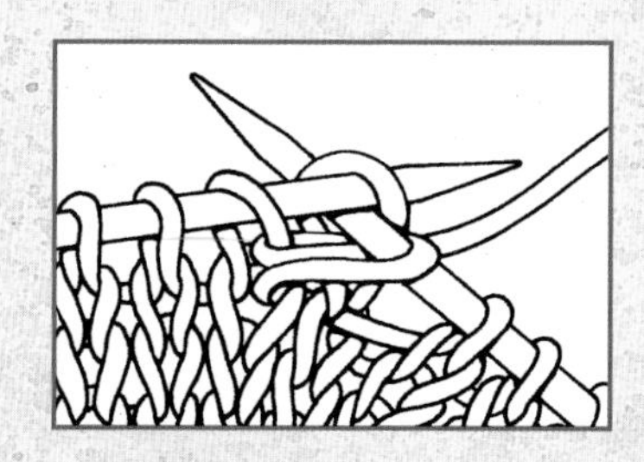

Working Through Back Loops

With yarn in back, insert the right needle into the **back** of the next stitch from **front** to **back** ***(Fig. 2)*** and knit it.

Fig. 2

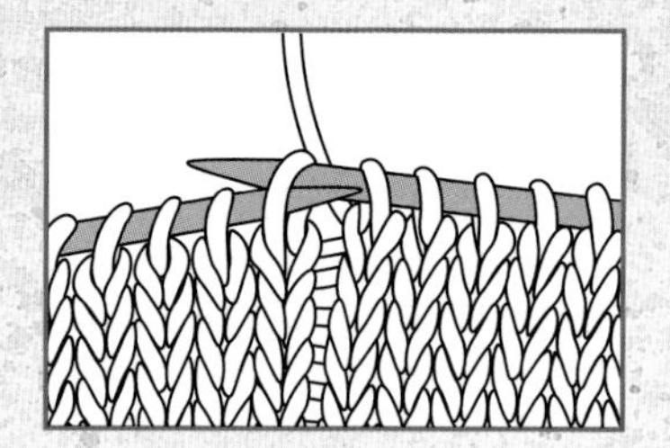

Yarn Over

Bring the yarn forward **between** the needles, then back **over** the top of the right hand needle, so that it is now in position to knit the next stitch ***(Fig. 3)***.

Fig. 3

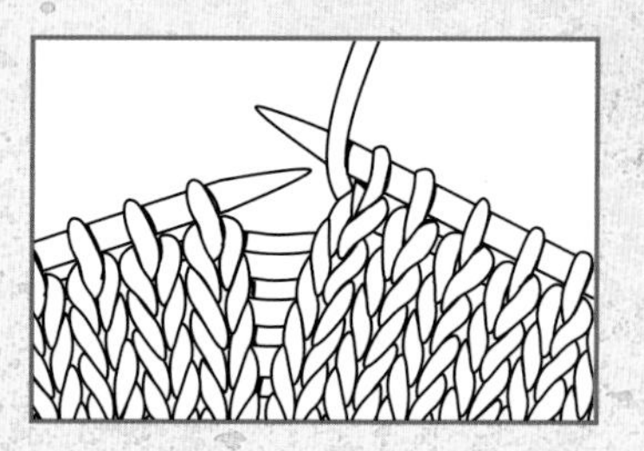

Increases

Make One *(abbreviated M1)*

Insert the **left** needle under the horizontal strand between the stitches from the front ***(Fig. 4a)***. Then knit into the **back** of the strand ***(Fig. 4b)***.

Fig. 4a

Fig. 4b

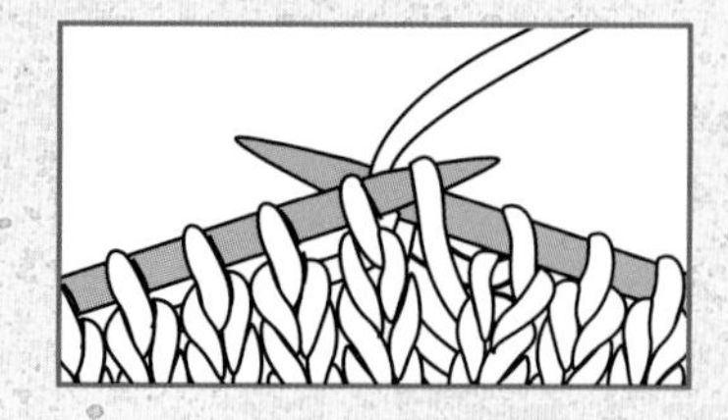

Left Invisible Increase

Insert the left needle from the **back** into the side of the stitch 2 rows **below** the stitch on the right needle ***(Fig. 5a)***, pull it up and knit into the back loop ***(Fig. 5b)***.

Fig. 5a

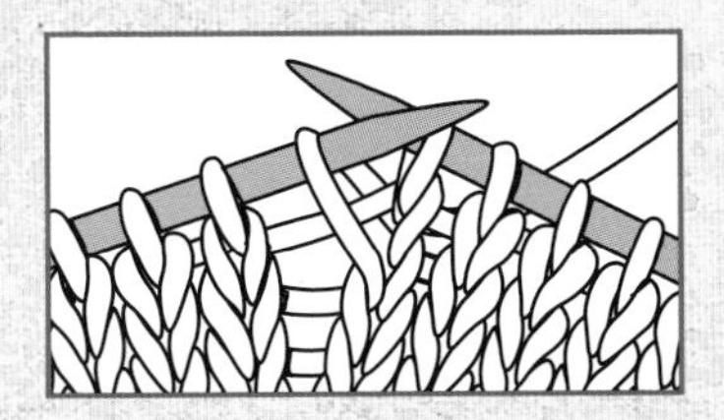

Fig. 5b

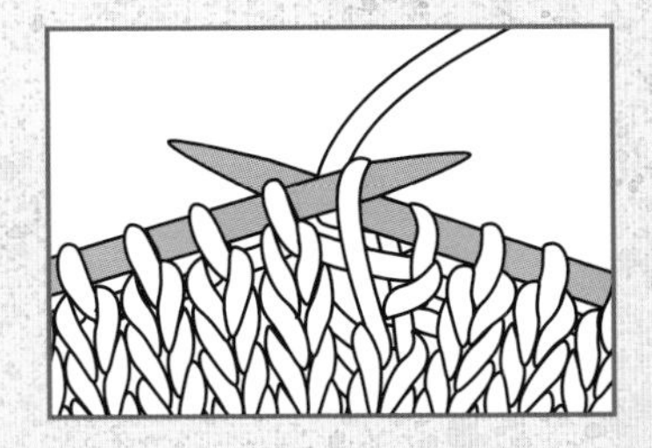

Right Invisible Increase

Insert the right needle from the **front** into the side of the stitch **below** the next stitch on the left needle ***(Fig. 6)***, and knit it.

Fig. 6

Knit Increase

Knit the next stitch but do **not** slip the old stitch off the left needle ***(Fig. 7a)***. Insert the right needle into the **back** loop of the same stitch and knit it ***(Fig. 7b)***, then slip the old stitch off the left needle.

Fig. 7a

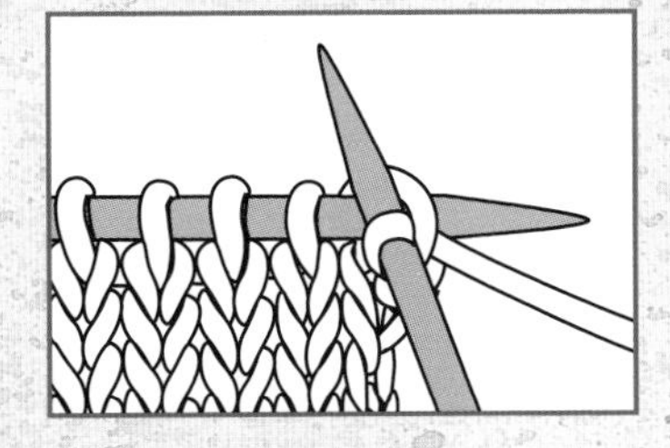

Fig. 7b

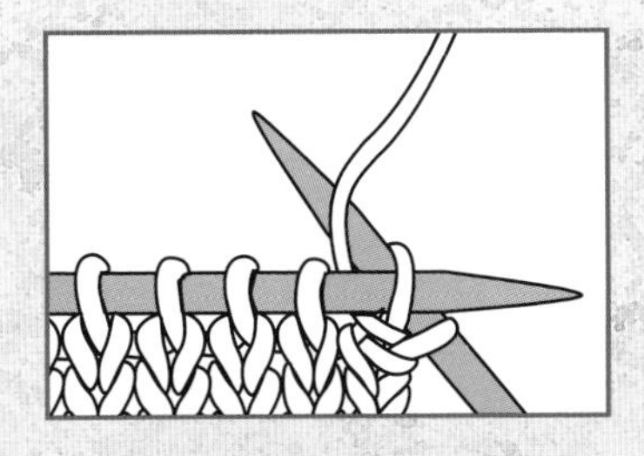

Purl Increase

Purl the next stitch but do not slip the old stitch off the left needle. Insert the right needle into the back loop of the same stitch from back to front ***(Fig. 8)*** and purl it. Slip the old stitch off the left needle.

Fig. 8

Decreases

Knit 2 Together

(abbreviated K2 tog)

Insert the right needle into the **front** of the first two stitches on the left needle as if to **knit** ***(Fig. 9)***, then **knit** them together as if they were one stitch.

Fig. 9

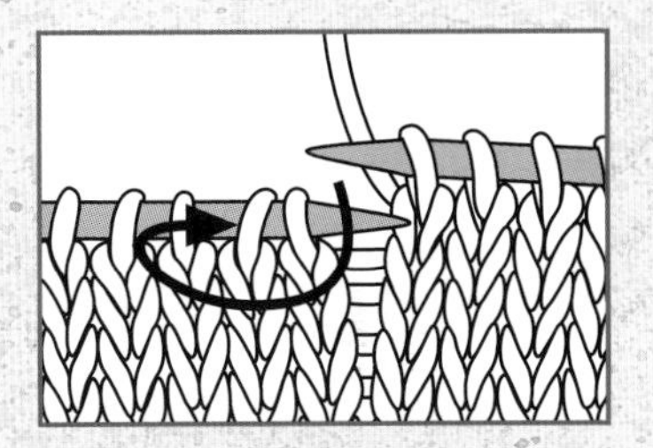

Knit 3 Together

(abbreviated K3 tog)

Insert the right needle into the **front** of the first three stitches on the left needle as if to **knit** ***(Fig. 10)***, then **knit** them together as if they were one stitch.

Fig. 10

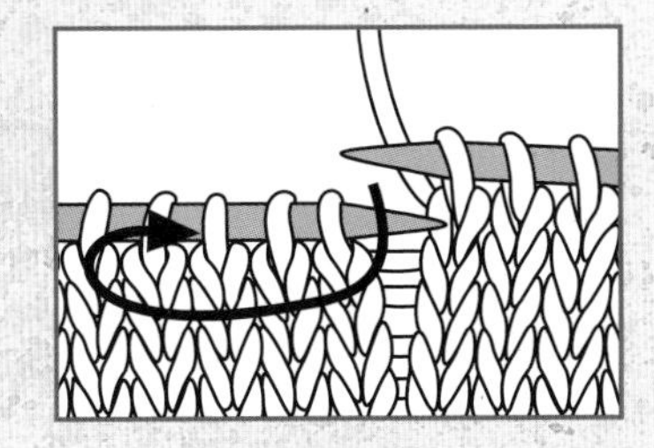

Slip 1, Knit 1, Pass Slipped Stitch Over

(abbreviated slip 1, K1, PSSO)

Slip one stitch as if to **knit** ***(Fig. 13a)***. Knit the next stitch. With the left needle, bring the slipped stitch over the knit stitch ***(Fig. 11)*** and off the needle.

Fig. 11

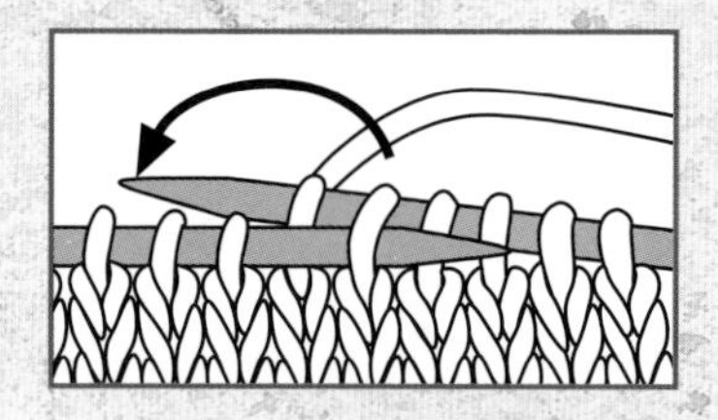

Slip, Slip, Knit

(abbreviated SSK)

Separately slip two stitches as if to **knit** ***(Fig. 12a)***. Insert the **left** needle into the **front** of both slipped stitches ***(Fig. 12b)*** and then **knit** them together as if they were one stitch ***(Fig. 12c)***.

Fig. 12a

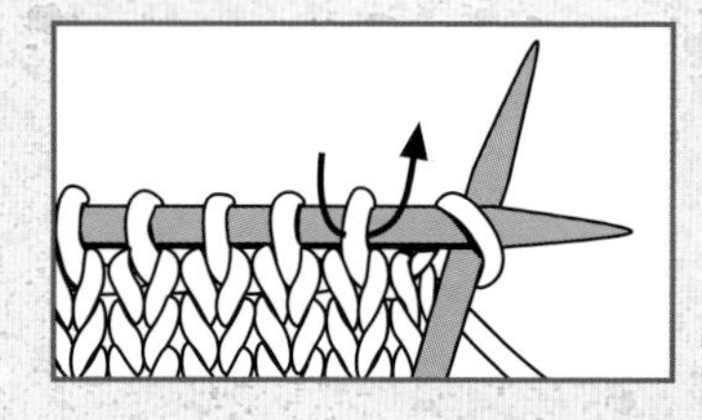

Fig. 12b

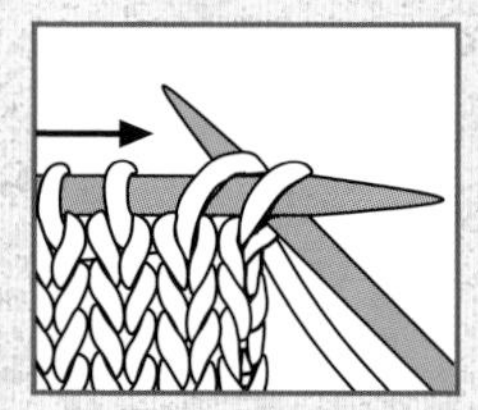

Fig. 12c

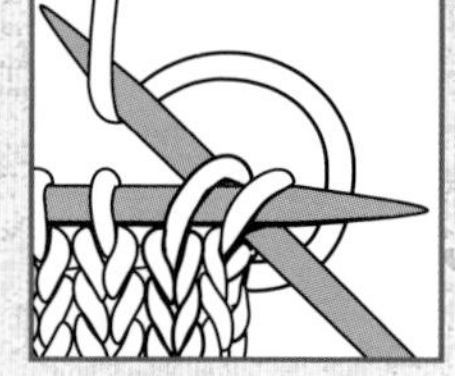

Slip 1, Knit 2 Together, Pass Slipped Stitch Over

(abbreviated slip 1, K2 tog, PSSO)

Slip one stitch as if to **knit** ***(Fig. 13a)***, then knit the next two stitches together. With the left needle, bring the slipped stitch over the stitch just made ***(Fig. 13b)*** and off the needle.

Fig. 13a

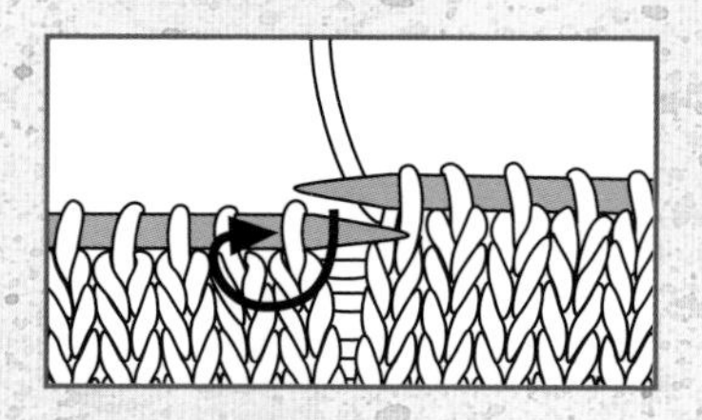

Fig. 13b

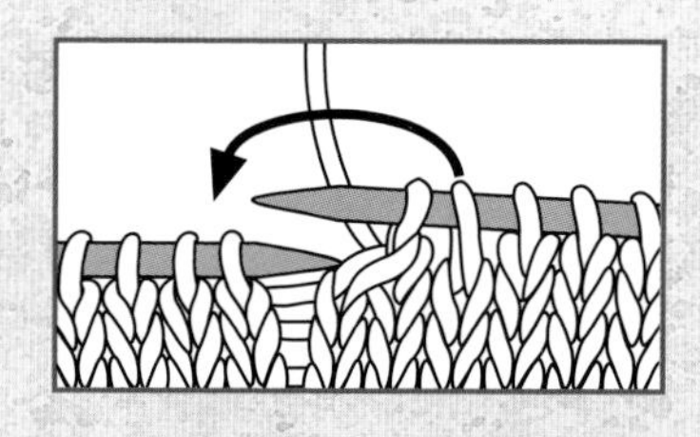

Slip 2, Knit 1, Pass 2 Slipped Stitches Over

(abbreviated slip 2, K1, P2SSO)

With yarn in back, slip two stitches together as if to knit ***(Fig. 14a)***, then knit the next stitch. With the left needle, bring both slipped stitches over the knit stitch ***(Fig. 14b)*** and off the needle.

Fig. 14a

Fig. 14b

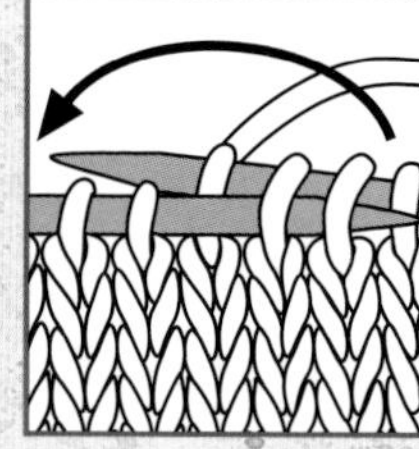

Purl 2 Together

(abbreviated P2 tog)

Insert the right needle into the **front** of the first two stitches on the left needle as if to **purl** ***(Fig. 15)***, then **purl** them together as if they were one stitch.

Fig. 15

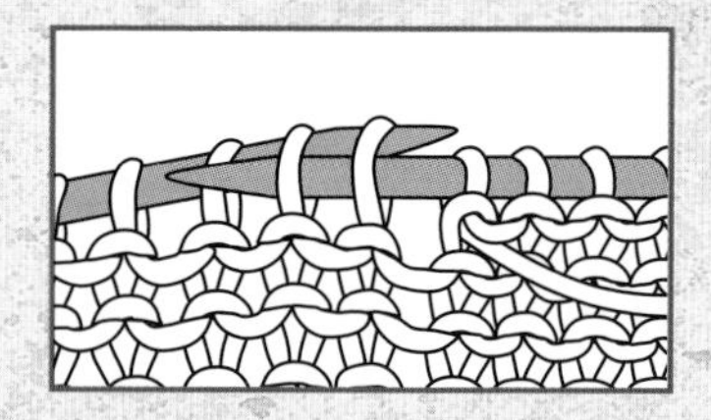

Purl 2 Together Through The Back Loop

(abbreviated P2 tog tbl)

Insert the right needle into the **back** of both stitches from **back** to **front** ***(Fig. 16)***, then **purl** them together as if they were one stitch

Fig. 16

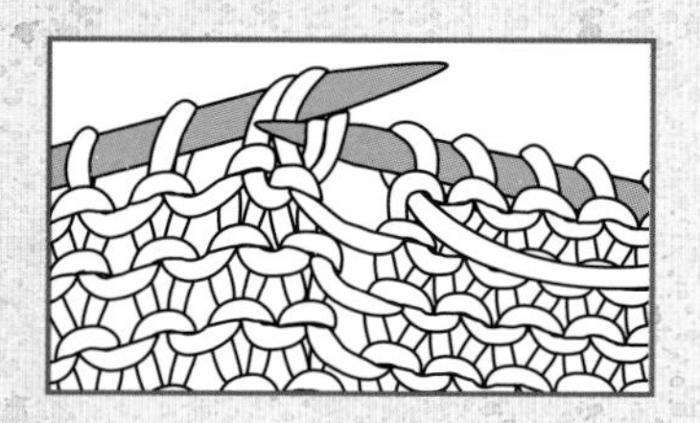

Circular Knitting

Using Circular Needle

When you knit a tube, as for the purse, you are going to work around on the outside of the circle, with the right side of the knitting facing you. Using a circular needle, cast on all stitches as instructed. Untwist and straighten the stitches on the needle to be sure that the cast on ridge lays on the inside of the needle and never rolls around the needle. Hold the needle so that the ball of yarn is attached to the stitch closest to the **right** hand point. Place a marker on the right hand point to mark the beginning of the round.

To begin working in the round, knit the stitches on the left hand point ***(Fig. 17)***.

Fig. 17

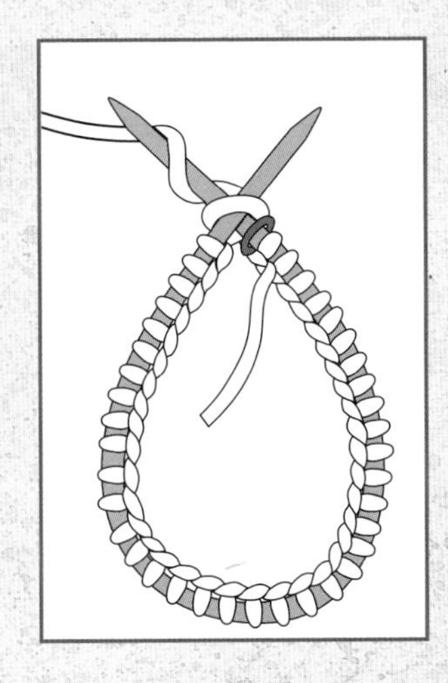

Continue working each round as instructed **without turning the work**; but for the first three rounds or so, check to be sure that the cast on edge has not twisted around the needle. If it has, it is impossible to untwist it. The only way to fix this is to rip it out and return to the cast on row.

Using Double Pointed Needles

When working too few stitches to use a circular needle, double pointed needles are required. Divide the stitches into fourths and slip one-fourth of the stitches onto each of 4 double pointed needles, forming a square ***(Fig. 18)***. With the fifth needle, knit across the stitches on the first needle. You will now have an empty needle with which to knit the stitches from the next needle. Work the first stitch of each needle firmly to prevent gaps.

Fig. 18

Changing Colors

When changing colors, always pick up the new color yarn from **beneath** the dropped yarn and keep the color which has just been worked to the left ***(Fig. 19)***. This will prevent holes in the finished piece. Take extra care to keep your tension even. Carry the unused yarn loosely along back of work.

Fig. 19

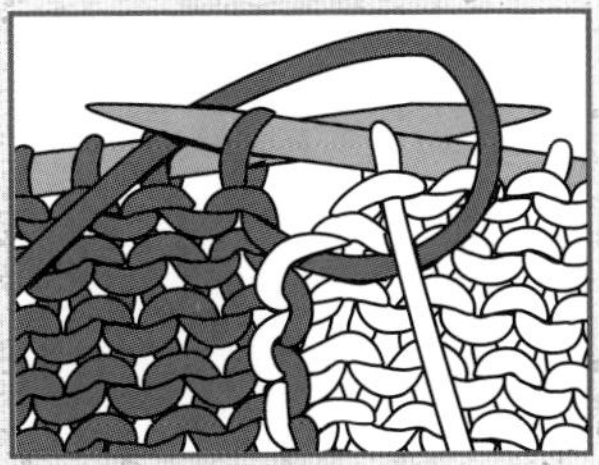

Adding New Stitches

Insert the right needle into stitch as if to **knit**, yarn over and pull loop through ***(Fig. 20a)***, insert the left needle into the loop just worked from **front** to **back** and slip the loop onto the left needle ***(Fig. 20b)***. Repeat for required number of stitches.

Fig. 20a

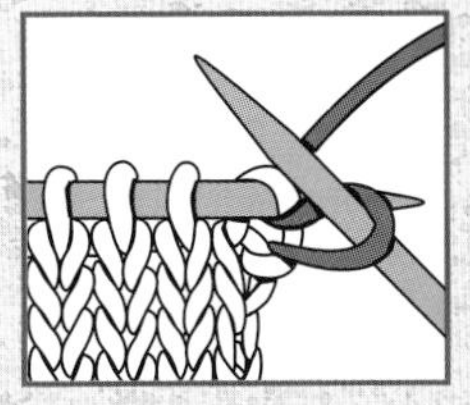

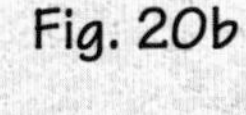

Fig. 20b

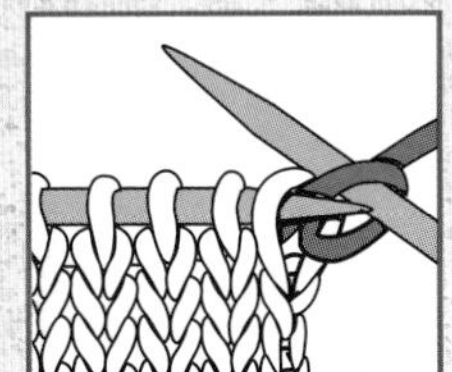

Picking Up Stitches

When instructed to pick up stitches, insert the needle from the **front** to the **back** under two strands at the edge of the worked piece ***(Figs. 21a & b)***. Put the yarn around the needle as if to **knit**, then bring the needle with the yarn back through the stitch to the right side, resulting in a stitch on the needle.

Repeat this along the edge, picking up the required number of stitches. A crochet hook may be helpful to pull yarn through.

Fig. 21a

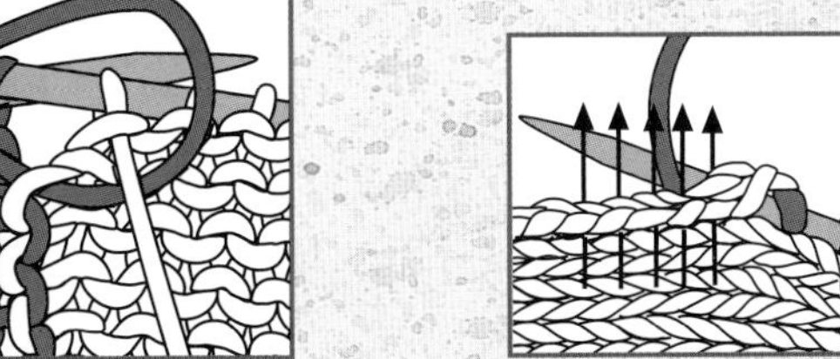

Fig. 21b

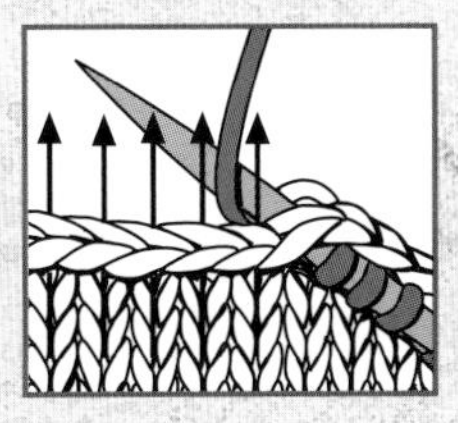

Weaving Seams

With the **right** side of both pieces facing you and edges even, sew through both sides once to secure the seam. Insert the needle under the bar **between** the first and second stitches on the row and pull the yarn through ***(Fig. 22)***. Insert the needle under the next bar on the second side. Repeat from side to side, being careful to match rows. If the edges are different lengths, it may be necessary to insert the needle under two bars at one edge.

Fig. 22

Felting Basics

Felting is simple, just 4 easy steps. All you are really doing is shrinking and changing the texture of your knitted project!

1. CHOOSING THE RIGHT YARN

Read the label. AVOID "superwash" wool or wool yarns labeled as machine washable as they are made, specifically, to NOT shrink. Be sure to choose a yarn that is at least 50% wool that will work to the gauge listed in the project instructions. **FYI:** White and light color yarns may not felt as well as heathers or darker colors.

2. KNIT YOUR PROJECT

ALWAYS make a test swatch. Swatch with all your yarns and colors to:

- Check knit gauge.
- Make sure all the yarns in the project felt the way you want them to. Even when you get the exact gauge called for before felting, washing machine agitation and water temperature will affect the amount of felting that occurs.
- Make sure colors do not run.

3. MACHINE FELT

Set your top-loading washing machine for a HOT wash and COLD rinse cycle. Add a tablespoon of detergent to the wash. Place the knitted project in a tight-mesh lingerie or sweater bag and toss into the machine. Throw in an **old** pair of jeans to speed up the felting process (the more agitation, the better). Check every 2-3 minutes during the wash cycle to keep an eye on size and shrinkage of the project. A properly felted project has shrunk to the desired size and the stitches are hard to see or have disappeared completely. When checking, you may want to wear rubber gloves to protect your hands from the hot water. It may be necessary to repeat the agitation cycle a second or third time. Once it's felted, remove it from the machine and allow the wash water to spin out. Put the project back in the washer for the cold rinse.

4. BLOCK (Shape and dry)

Roll the felted item in a towel and gently squeeze out the excess water. Don't wring the towel as that may set in permanent creases. Form it into the size and shape by pinning to a blocking board or placing over an object the size and shape you want your finished object to be. Let your project air dry even though it may take several days.

Embroidery Stitches

Backstitch

The backstitch is worked from **right** to **left**. Come up at 1, go down at 2 and come up at 3 ***(Fig. 23)***. The second stitch is made by going down at 1 and coming up at 4.

Fig. 23

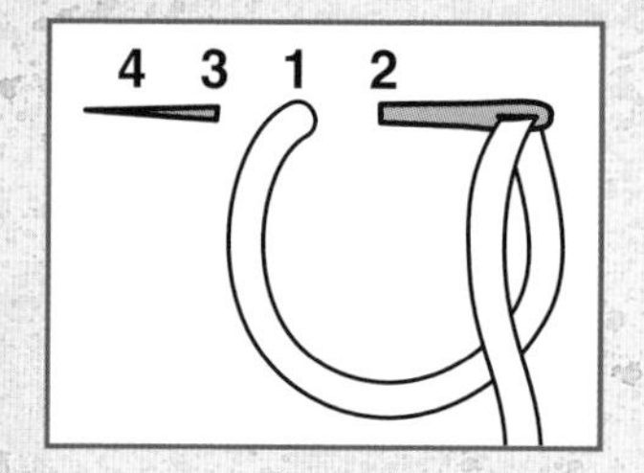

Straight Stitch

Straight Stitch is just what the name implies, a single, straight stitch. Come up at 1 and go down at 2 ***(Fig. 24)***.

Fig. 24

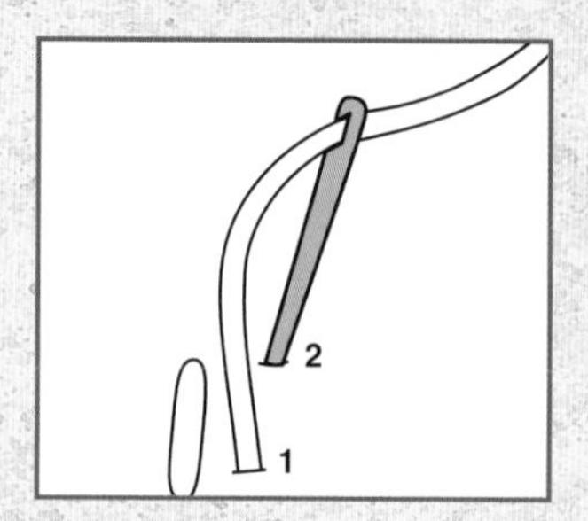

Yarn Information

The projects in this leaflet were made with various weights of yarn. Any brand of yarn may be used. It is best to refer to the yardage/meters when determining how many balls or skeins to purchase. Remember, to arrive at the finished size, it is the GAUGE/TENSION that is important, not the brand of yarn.

For your convenience, listed below are yarns used to create our photography models.

Felted Purse
Patons® Classic Merino Wool
Blue - #00215 Blue Storm
Red - #00207 Rich Red
Teal - #00218 Peacock
Green - #00240 Leaf Green
Gold - #00204 Old Gold

Clutch
Lion Brand® Lion Wool
Orange - #133 Pumpkin
Variegated - #201 Autumn Sunset

Textured Purse
Lion Brand® Wool-Ease® Chunky
#402 Wheat

Textured Stripes Afghan
TLC® Essentials™
Lt Teal - #2820 Robin Egg
Green - #2615 Lt Celery
TLC® Heathers™
Dk Teal - #2470 Teal

Dog Sweater
Patons® Shetland Chunky Tweed
#67532 Deep Red

Flowered Stole
Patons® Décor
Brown - #01632 Rich Taupe
Green - #01636 Sage Green
Tan - #01631 Taupe
Mauve - #01625 Pale Aubergine

Hat
Bernat® Softee® Chunky
Green - #39236 Medium Sea Green
Red Heart® Strata™
#8528 Cascade

Mittens
Red Heart® Strata™
#8528 Cascade

Toe Up Socks
Moda Dea® Washable Wool™
Green - #4440 Moss
Purple - #4431 Plum

Blue Booties
Patons® Grace
Blue - #60130 Sky

Pink Booties
Patons® Grace
Pink - #60146 Blush

Teddy Bear
Moda Dea® Tweedle Dee™
#8901 Sahara
Patons® Astra
#02873 Tan
Lion Brand® Homespun®
#326 Ranch

Production Team

Instructional Editor
Joan Beebe

Editorial Writer
Susan McManus Johnson

Graphic Artist
Jeanne Zaffarano

Senior Graphic Artist
Lora Puls

Photo Stylists
Anne Pulliam Stocks
Becky Werle

Photographer
Mark Matthews

We have made every effort to ensure that these instructions are accurate and complete. We cannot, however, be responsible for human error, typographical mistakes, or variations in individual work.

Items made and instructions tested by Sue Galucki, Raymelle Greening, and Kitty Jo Pietzuch.